MIND YOUR BUSINESS

The Blueprint to Black Wealth

by John J

ABOUT THE AUTHOR

Before I became a digital activist, writer, and motivational coach, I had been through various challenging situations. I was starving and homeless and was even incarcerated. It was a struggle that many people haven't been able to overcome. Being a product of my environment and realizing its effect on me since childhood, I started to aspire for a better situation for my community. While I know it is not easy not having money or a job and support system that encourages you, I am here to show you that you can succeed. I understand that many factors make it hard to get out of a bad situation, but I intend to serve as your motivation.

JOHN J

INTRODUCTION

FINANCIAL LITERACY IS THE KEY TO A PROSPEROUS AND STABLE FINANCIAL FUTURE FOR EVERYONE, REGARDLESS OF RACE OR ETHNICITY. UNFORTUNATELY, FOR MANY BLACK PEOPLE IN THE UNITED STATES, ACCESS TO FINANCIAL EDUCATION AND RESOURCES HAS BEEN LIMITED, CONTRIBUTING TO A STAGGERING WEALTH GAP THAT PERSISTS TO THIS DAY. IT IS TIME TO ACKNOWLEDGE THIS INEQUALITY AND TAKE ACTION.

As someone whose life experiences have developed to assist and empower people in achieving their financial goals, I am honored to introduce this book about financial literacy for Black people in the U.S. This book has been created to help close the racial gap in financial literacy and empower Black people to take control of their finances, build wealth, and achieve their dreams.

Inside these pages, you will find a comprehensive guide to financial literacy covering various topics relevant to the Black community. From budgeting, saving, investing, and retirement planning, you will discover strategies and advice for managing money and building wealth here.

INTODUCTION (CONT)

FINANCIAL LITERACY IS NOT JUST ABOUT NUMBERS AND FINANCIAL STRATEGIES. IT ALSO ADDRESSES THE SYSTEMIC BARRIERS THAT HAVE PREVENTED BLACK PEOPLE FROM ACCESSING FINANCIAL RESOURCES AND BUILDING WEALTH. THIS BOOK DISCUSSES THE HISTORICAL AND SOCIAL CONTEXTS THAT CONTRIBUTE TO THE RACIAL WEALTH GAP IN THE U.S. AND STRATEGIES FOR OVERCOMING THESE CHALLENGES AND MAKING A MORE JUST AND EQUITABLE FINANCIAL SYSTEM.

WHETHER YOU ARE JUST STARTING YOUR MONETARY MISSION OR LOOKING TO ADD TO YOUR EXISTING KNOWLEDGE AND SKILLS. THIS BOOK IS FOR YOU. IT WILL SERVE AS A VALUABLE RESOURCE AND ENCOURAGE YOU TO TAKE CONTROL OF YOUR FINANCES AND ACHIEVE YOUR DREAMS. TOGETHER. WE CAN CLOSE THE RACIAL WEALTH GAP AND BUILD A BETTER FINANCIAL FUTURE FOR EVERYONE.

Black people's economic disparities in the United States have a long and complex history rooted in systemic racism and inequality. From slavery, when Black people were forcibly brought to the United States as chattel, to the Jim Crow era, during which discriminatory laws and policies were enacted to segregate and marginalize Black people, the barriers to economic progress and wealth accumulation for Black people have been significant.

Even after the civil rights movement of the 1960s, when legal segregation was abolished and voting rights secured, economic inequality persisted. Redlining, denying financial services to Black neighborhoods, kept Black people from accessing home mortgages and other forms of capital necessary to build wealth, exacerbating the racial wealth gap.

The extreme increase in mass incarceration in the 1980s and 1990s disproportionately affected Black people, leading to a cycle of poverty and disadvantage that further entrenched economic disparities. Despite some progress in closing the racial wealth gap, the median net worth of Black households is still less than one-tenth that of white families.

01. UNDERSTANDING PERSONAL FINANCES

Personal finances refer to the governing of an individual's monetary situation. This includes income, expenses, investments, and debt. Managing one's finances effectively is crucial for achieving financial security and freedom. It requires discipline, planning, and informed decision-making. Managing personal finances effectively can lead to financial stress, debt, and limited opportunities.

BUDGETING EXPENSES

Budgeting is a vital aspect of personal finance management. It is creating a plan for how an individual intends to spend their money over a specific period. Creating a budget helps individuals prioritize their spending, avoid overspending, and save more. Individuals must identify their income, fixed and variable expenses, and savings goals to create a budget. Budgeting software, mobile applications, or simple spreadsheets can help track and manage costs.

TRACKING INVESTMENTS

Tracking expenses, such as food, transportation, utilities, and entertainment, provides valuable insights into how individuals spend their money daily. By monitoring their costs, individuals can identify areas where they overspend or spend unnecessarily and adjust accordingly. Tracking expenses using various tools, including budgeting apps and expense-tracking spreadsheets.

By keeping track of expenses and creating a budget, individuals can gain greater control over their finances and build long-term wealth. It helps avoid debt by making conscious decisions about how to spend the available resources. Mastering budgeting and tracking expenses ultimately empowers individuals to make informed financial decisions, improve their health, and meet financial goals.

Tracking expenses, such as food, transportation, utilities, and entertainment, provides valuable insights into how individuals spend their money daily. By monitoring their costs, individuals can identify areas where they overspend or spend unnecessarily and adjust accordingly. Tracking expenses using various tools, including budgeting apps and expense-tracking spreadsheets.

CREDIT SCORES AND REPORTS

Credit scores and reports are essential components of personal finance management. A credit score is a numerical representation of an individual's creditworthiness or financial health. Lenders use the credit score to determine an individual's creditworthiness, that is, their ability to repay loans or credit card debts. Personal Credit points range from 300 to 850, with higher scores representing better creditworthiness.

On the other hand, credit reports are detailed records of an individual's credit history. They show credit card balances, loan balances, payment history, and additional relevant information. Lenders use credit reports to review an individual's credit history when deciding whether to lend to them.

Understanding credit scores and reports are critical for managing personal finances effectively. By regularly reviewing their credit report, an individual can identify errors, detect fraud, and prevent identity theft. A good credit score can increase their chances of obtaining loans, credit cards, and other financial products with favorable terms and conditions. Monitoring credit scores regularly and maintaining a good credit history by paying bills on time, avoiding excessive credit utilization, and reducing outstanding debts is essential. By understanding and improving their credit scores and reports, individuals can take control of their financial future and achieve financial freedom.

MANAGING YOUR DEBT

Managing debt is a critical aspect of personal finance management. Debt can be a valuable tool for making major purchases, such as a home or car, but it can also be a source of financial stress and anxiety. Effective debt management requires a clear understanding of one's financial situation, the terms and conditions of the loans, and a repayment plan. Prioritizing high-interest debts and focusing on paying them off first is essential.

To manage debt effectively, individuals should avoid excessive debt and limit spending on credit cards. They should also consider consolidating debts into a single lender or credit card with a lower interest rate. This can make it easier to manage payments and save on interest charges. If an individual is struggling to manage their debt, they should consider seeking the assistance of a financial advisor or credit counseling service. With the right approach and tools, anyone can improve their debt management skills and achieve financial stability. Individuals can reduce financial stress, improve credit scores, and achieve financial freedom by taking control of debt.

SAVING FOR EMERGENCIES AND RETIREMENT

Saving for emergencies and retirement is a crucial aspect of personal finance management. Emergencies such as job loss, medical challenges, or unexpected repair bills can happen anytime. Building an emergency fund, usually, three to six months of living expenses, can provide a cushion during tough times. The emergency fund helps individuals stay afloat during emergencies, avoid going into debt or dipping into retirement savings, and alleviate financial stress. Setting up an automatic savings plan or a separate savings account focused on emergency savings is critical.

Retirement savings also require careful planning and consistent, long-term efforts. Individuals can start by planning for their retirement goals, estimating the amount of money they need to save, and then set a timeline and target savings amount. An individual's retirement savings plan should start early to ensure compounding growth. Consistent investment in retirement plans such as 401(k), Individual Retirement Account (IRA), or Roth IRA can help individuals maximize their retirement savings. Advisors can help guide individuals through investment strategies that offer tax benefits or suggest other financial instruments that align with their goals. Individuals can secure a comfortable future and live stress-free during their golden years by starting early and regularly.

02. BUILDING THROUGH INVESTING

THE POWER OF INVESTING

Investing is a powerful tool for building wealth and achieving long-term financial goals. Investing involves putting money into financial products such as stocks, real estate, or mutual funds to generate a return on investment (ROI). One of the main advantages of investing is that it offers the potential for earning a more lucrative rate of return than savings accounts or other conservative options. Investing in a portfolio that includes a mix of different investment types further reduces risk and can achieve higher returns over time.

Investing requires careful research and understanding of the markets and how they operate. However, investing is not only for the wealthy or the financial elite. New digital investment platforms and robo-advisors offer an affordable and accessible way for anyone to start investing with minimum investment amounts. By investing consistently and strategically, individuals can earn a significant return on their investment, build wealth, and achieve their long-term financial goals. However, seeking advice from professional financial advisors to minimize the risk and maximize the rewards is essential. With the right investment plan and patience, anyone can harness investing's power to secure their financial future.

STOCKS, BONDS, AND FUNDS

Stocks, bonds, and funds are three essential investment vehicles for individuals looking to diversify their investment portfolio. Stocks, also known as equities, represent shares of ownership in a publicly traded company. When individuals invest in stocks, they hope to earn returns through rising stock prices and potential dividend income. Stocks can offer high returns, but they inherently come with higher risk.

Bonds, on the other hand, are debt instruments issued by corporations and government entities. When individuals buy bonds, they lend money to the bond issuer in return for interest payments and the return on the principal investment. Bonds offer lower returns than stocks but are generally considered safer investments. Mutual funds and exchange-traded funds (ETFs) aggregate money from individual investors to invest in various financial products such as stocks, bonds, and other securities. Funds offer diversification while minimizing risk by spreading investments across different asset classes.

Understanding the benefits and risks of each investment vehicle is crucial before making investment decisions. Individuals should research these investment products, consider their goals, and consult with investment professionals to make informed investment decisions. Ultimately, individuals can achieve their long-term financial goals and build wealth by diversifying their investment portfolio and investing consistently and strategically.

DEVELOPING AN INVESTMENT STRATEGY

Developing an investment strategy ensures individuals achieve their financial goals most effectively. The first step is to assess personal financial goals, risk tolerance, and investment horizon. Based on these factors, an individual can develop an investment plan that aligns with their investment objectives, such as capital appreciation, income, or long-term growth.

Diversification is a vital aspect of any investment strategy. It means spreading investments across different asset classes, sectors, and geographical regions. This reduces the impact of any one investment performing poorly and helps maximize returns while minimizing risks. Regular portfolio rebalancing is crucial to maintain diversification and reduce exposure to market risks. It is essential to routinely monitor the performance of investments, seek professional advice, and stay informed about the financial markets changing dynamics. Individuals can build wealth and achieve long-term economic prosperity by developing a thoughtful and strategic investment plan and sticking to it consistently.

INVESTING FOR RETIREMENT

Investing for retirement is a crucial aspect of personal finance management. Individuals must start saving and investing as early as possible to ensure they have enough money for retirement. Most retirement investments are long-term investments that feature compounding interest or dividends. Protecting through a 401(k), 403(b), Traditional IRA or Roth IRA, and other retirement savings vehicles are standard ways for individuals to save for retirement.

Retirement investing also necessitates a conservative investment approach prioritizing long-term security over high short-term gains. While it is a good idea to diversify a retirement investment portfolio across various asset classes, maintaining an allocation in 'safe' investment products, such as government- or investment-grade bonds, becomes increasingly critical as retirement approaches. Individuals should consider seeking professional advice or using services offered by investment advisors with experience managing retirement accounts. Individuals can build a secure and comfortable retirement by starting early, developing a consistent investment plan, and seeking the appropriate guidance.

RISK AND BENEFITS OF INVESTING

Investing, like any financial activity, comes with its risks and benefits. Investing involves the possibility of losing money due to market fluctuations, company-specific risks, or economic conditions. In some cases, investments may not perform as expected, resulting in lower returns or a loss. Understanding the risks of investing and developing strategies to manage them is essential.

Despite these risks, investing provides numerous opportunities for wealth creation, income generation, and capital appreciation. A well-diversified investment portfolio can help reduce risk and generate attractive returns over the long run. Investing in a company's stock can offer the potential for appreciation in share value and dividends while investing in bonds can provide regular income through fixed-interest payments. Moreover, investing can help individuals achieve long-term financial goals, such as retirement, college education, and home ownership.

Individuals should invest after carefully considering the risks and seeking appropriate professional advice. Risk tolerance, investment goals, and other personal factors can impact investment decisions. It is crucial to have a long-term investment strategy, monitor investments regularly, and remain informed about market trends and economic conditions. With a thoughtful and knowledgeable approach to investing, individuals can enjoy the benefits of wealth creation and achieve their long-term financial goals.

03. STRATEGIES FOR FINANCIAL SUCCESS

STARTING A SMALL BUSINESS

Starting a small business can be a gratifying and rewarding experience, but it requires creativity, persistence, and careful planning. The first step is identifying a unique product or service idea based on market demand or personal interests. Then, assess the target market, competitive landscape, and regulatory requirements to ensure the business idea is viable.

Once the feasibility has been established, a comprehensive business plan that covers the business goals, marketing and branding strategy, revenue streams, and financial needs should be created. Having adequate financial resources or investors to fund the start-up period and cover expenses until profits roll in is essential. More importantly, entrepreneurs should understand the legal and financial aspects of starting a business. Compliance with tax laws, licenses, and zoning regulations is crucial to avoid legal issues and financial distress later. By pursuing their passion, developing a well-thought-out plan, and seeking professional guidance, individuals can embark on a fulfilling entrepreneurship journey and realize their business dreams.

NAVIGATING WORKPLACE POLITICS FOR FINANCIAL GAIN

Navigating workplace politics can be a delicate balance between gaining strategic advantages and avoiding detrimental consequences. It is often inevitable that workplace politics exist in any organization. Still, a proper understanding of office politics and navigating them can benefit financial gains, career advancement, and overall job satisfaction.

The key to effectively navigating office politics is maintaining professional conduct, remaining objective, and focusing on achieving long-term financial gains. To do this, it's advisable to avoid conflicts and gossip, uphold high ethical standards, and keep all lines of communication open. By building strong working relationships with teammates and superiors, individuals can develop alliances to help them navigate challenging situations and cultivate opportunities for financial gain. Moreover, networking with colleagues across different departments and workgroups can offer valuable insights into the organization's inner workings and inform strategic decisions that benefit an individual's financial gains. Ultimately, a careful and thoughtful approach can help individuals navigate workplace politics while strengthening their position financially and improving their overall success in the organization.

UNDERSTANDING AND NEGOTIATING CONTRACTS

Understanding and negotiating contracts are essential skills for personal finance and business management. Contracts are legal documents that define the terms and conditions of a transaction or agreement between two or more parties. Whether it's a rental lease, employment contract, or partnership agreement, understanding the terms of the contract is critical to ensuring that both parties agree on the responsibilities and obligations.

When negotiating contracts, individuals should thoroughly review the contract's terms and seek legal counsel if necessary. They should ensure that the words are fair and reasonable, and if not, negotiate for better terms or compensation. Additionally, individuals should be aware of hidden fees, penalties, or conditions and seek clarification from the contracting party before signing the contract. Negotiating a contract can help individuals avoid unforeseen costs, infringements on their rights, or loss of financial benefits.

By understanding and negotiating contracts, individuals can protect their financial interests, enter into agreements confidently, and minimize the risk of unforeseen financial losses or expenses. It is an essential component of personal finance and business management that requires attention to detail, communication skills, and a keen sense of fairness and ethics.

INVESTING IN EDUCATION/PROFESSIONAL DEVELOPMENT

Investing in education and professional development can provide numerous benefits, including career advancement, higher income, and expanded opportunities for financial growth. Additional education or professional development training can improve an individual's skill set, broaden their knowledge base, and enhance their network of contacts in the industry. These benefits can lead to significant financial gains, job satisfaction, and a competitive edge in the job market.

Investing in education or professional development requires both financial and time commitments. Individuals should research the options that best fit their goals, budget, and availability. Many options include online courses, in-person classes, workshops, and conferences. Sometimes, employers offer their employees educational opportunities, training programs, or tuition reimbursement. Individuals can also consult career advisors, financial planners, or industry professionals to help guide their choices. By investing in education and professional development, individuals can take advantage of new opportunities, gain the skills and knowledge to reach their goals and build a secure and prosperous financial future.

04. CONQUERING DAY-TO-DAY FINANCIAL CHALLENGES

TACKLING STUDENT LOANS

Student loans can be a heavy burden for many people. However, several ways to tackle student loans and manage them effectively exist. One strategy is to create a budget and stick to it. Setting financial goals and being disciplined with spending makes it easier to allocate funds toward paying off student loans. Additionally, exploring repayment options such as income-driven repayment plans or loan forgiveness programs is essential. These options make monthly payments more manageable and provide long-term relief from student loan debt.

ACCESSING AFFORDABLE HOUSING

Accessing affordable housing can be a challenge for many individuals and families. One strategy is to research local and federal housing programs that provide affordable housing options. These programs are designed to assist low-income households and provide financial assistance to make housing more affordable. For example, Section 8 vouchers provide rental services to qualifying individuals and families, while the Low Income Home Energy Assistance Program (LIHEAP) delivers help with utility bills.

(Refer to: Inter-County Community Council | Energy Assistance. https://intercountycc.org/services/energy-assistance/)

Another strategy is to explore innovative housing solutions such as co-housing or house-sharing arrangements. These arrangements involve several individuals or families sharing a home or apartment and splitting the rent and utilities. This can significantly reduce housing costs and provide a supportive community for individuals and families. Additionally, consider looking for affordable housing farther away from city centers. While this may require a longer commute, saving money on rent or mortgage payments can be effective. Accessing affordable housing requires creative thinking and a willingness to explore different options. By leveraging housing programs and exploring non-traditional housing arrangements, it's possible to secure affordable housing and improve overall financial stability.

Another strategy is to increase your income through side hustles or freelance work. Taking on additional work can generate extra cash that can be allocated toward paying off student loans. Additionally, making extra payments towards your principal balance can help reduce interest charges and shorten the loan term. This can be achieved by increasing monthly expenses or making lump sum payments. Overall, tackling student loan debt requires a proactive approach and a willingness to make financial sacrifices. With dedication and perseverance, it's possible to overcome student loan debt and achieve financial freedom.

CREATING STRATEGIES TO SAVE FOR MAJOR PURCHASES

Saving for significant purchases such as a car, home, or vacation can be challenging. However, creating a savings plan and sticking to it can help achieve those goals. One strategy is to set SMART (specific, measurable, attainable, relevant, and time-bound) goals for the purchase. Doing so allows you to break the savings goal into smaller, more manageable chunks that you can work towards regularly. For example, if you are economizing and saving for a $20,000 motorcycle, you can set a plan to save $1000 per month for 20 months. This approach ensures you work towards a specific target and can track progress to make necessary adjustments.

Another strategy is to reduce expenses wherever possible. Take a hard look at your costs and determine which can be cut back or eliminated. You can free up additional funds towards your savings goal by reducing expenses. Additionally, consider setting up automatic savings transfers to a dedicated savings account. This way, a portion of your income is automatically deposited into savings each month, making savings a priority. Finally, take into account the power of minor additions to savings. Every little bit counts, so eliminate unnecessary purchases such as a daily coffee or eating out and add those small savings to your larger savings goal. By utilizing these strategies and staying disciplined, you can save for major purchases and achieve your financial goals.

NAVIGATING HEALTHCARE COST

Navigating healthcare costs can be a daunting task. One strategy is researching available healthcare plans and services to find one that meets your needs and budget. Whether you are selecting a plan through your employer or purchasing insurance through the healthcare marketplace, review each project's details and compare each's cost and coverage. Additionally, consider using online resources to compare the cost of medical procedures from different providers. These resources can help you find high-quality care at a more affordable price.

Another strategy is to practice preventative care to keep healthcare costs down in the long run. This includes scheduling regular check-ups, receiving recommended screenings, and maintaining a healthy lifestyle. By catching health problems early and taking preventative measures, you can avoid costly medical treatments and procedures down the road. Finally, if you receive a medical bill that is too high to manage, feel free to negotiate with your healthcare provider or ask for payment plan options. Many providers are willing to work with patients to find affordable payment options. Overall, navigating healthcare costs requires diligence and a willingness to take charge of your healthcare expenses. Being proactive and informed can minimize healthcare costs and maintain overall well-being.

CHAPTER 5: COMMUNITY WEALTH-BUILDING

CREATING WEALTH WITHIN BLACK COMMUNITIES

Creating wealth within Black communities has been a challenge for many years. One effective strategy is to support Black-owned businesses. Buying products and services from Black-owned companies promotes economic growth within the community and provides access to a broader range of goods and services. Supporting Black-owned businesses can also help create community jobs, leading to more financial stability and growth.

Another strategy is to invest in education and entrepreneurship programs. Programs that support education and entrepreneurship can provide valuable resources and strategies for individuals looking to create wealth within their communities. These programs offer to learn about financial literacy, business creation, and investment. By investing in these programs, individuals can gain the knowledge and skills to create and grow successful businesses and personal finance portfolios. Ultimately, creating wealth within Black communities requires a multifaceted approach that involves supporting Black-owned businesses and investing in education and entrepreneurship. We can take significant steps toward creating financial stability and prosperity by working together.

POOLING RESOURCES

Black people pooling resources to support investing, entrepreneurship, and community development can significantly change economic growth and job creation. By pooling resources, community members can provide support and funding for individual and community projects that would otherwise be difficult to achieve. This approach can generate wealth within the community and support local businesses, creating job opportunities and increasing economic stability.

One strategy for pooling resources is to form investment clubs or cooperatives. These groups allow individuals to combine resources and invest in larger projects, such as buying property, launching a new business, or funding community development initiatives. Additionally, resources can be pooled to provide seed funding for entrepreneurs and small businesses. This approach can help create job opportunities while promoting local business growth. Furthermore, pooling resources can enhance community development initiatives, such as building community centers, parks, or affordable housing, making the community more resilient, connected, and prosperous.

Overall, pooling resources is a powerful strategy for Black people interested in investing, entrepreneurship, and community development. It allows the community to address economic challenges and develop solutions that fit the specific needs and priorities of the community. By fostering a spirit of collaboration, mutual support, and trust among community members, this approach can generate significant benefits for individuals, businesses, and the community.

SUPPORTING BLACK-OWNED BUSINESSES

Black-owned businesses are a necessary part of the economy and play a significant role in creating jobs and driving economic growth within the community. By supporting Black-owned businesses, we can help to promote social and economic justice, build wealth in Black communities, and create opportunities for future generations.
One of the most productive ways to assist Black-owned businesses is to seek them out and purchase goods and services intentionally. This approach can make a significant difference in the success and growth of Black-owned businesses. Additionally, we can amplify Black-owned companies on social media, leave positive reviews, and recommend them to family and friends. By increasing visibility for Black-owned businesses, we can create a culture of support and success that benefits everyone. Supporting Black-owned businesses is essential to creating a more equitable and just society. By intentionally supporting Black-owned businesses, we can help produce a better future for our communities and their members.

INVESTING IN COMMUNITY-BASED PROJECTS

Understand the importance of investing in community-based projects. Community-based projects are initiatives that address the needs of a specific community, such as improving public spaces, providing access to fresh food, or developing affordable housing. When community members invest in these projects, they can create meaningful change within their neighborhoods and create long-term benefits for the community.

One strategy for investing in community-based projects is to join a community development corporation (CDC). CDCs are non-profit organizations dedicated to addressing a specific community's needs. By joining a CDC, you can have a voice in shaping community development initiatives and contribute to projects that are important to your community. Additionally, consider participating in crowdfunding campaigns that support community-based projects. Crowdfunding campaigns allow individuals to contribute directly to community-based projects, such as building a community center or developing a public garden. By contributing to these campaigns, you can have a tangible impact on the development of your community.

Investing in community-based projects is vital to creating thriving and equitable communities. By getting involved in CDCs or supporting crowdfunding campaigns, individuals can contribute to the development of their community and create long-term benefits that will improve the lives of all community members. By working together and investing in the future of our communities, we can create a better world for ourselves and future generations.

CONCLUSION

Financial stability is critical for achieving long-term security and is essential for building intergenerational wealth that can be passed down to future generations. Therefore, Black individuals and families must take control of their finances and make informed decisions that will benefit their future.

LEAVE YOUR EMAIL ADDRESS @ WWW.ADBMSTATEOFMIND.COM

CALL TO ACTION

To take control of our finances, Black people can start by educating themselves on personal finance topics such as budgeting, investing, and managing debt. They can also look for financial advisors or resources that cater to their specific needs and are sensitive to their unique financial circumstances. Additionally, Black people can explore alternative sources of funding and investment that offer alternatives to traditional institutions that may have been historically discriminatory.

Taking control of our finances requires a proactive approach and a willingness to learn and explore new financial opportunities. By educating themselves and engaging with resources that cater to their specific needs and circumstances, Black people can create a more stable and prosperous future for themselves and their families. They can build intergenerational wealth and create a more equitable society by making informed financial decisions.

RESOURCES FOR ADDITIONAL FINANCIAL EDUCATION/SUPPORT

These resources have been developed to create an inclusive environment for Black individuals to gain information and services to support their financial wellness.

Firstly, the Financial Gym is a financial planning company dedicated to creating resources and financial education opportunities for Black individuals. They provide online tools, personalized support, and financial coaching designed to precisely meet Black individuals' needs. Their mission is to use education to empower individuals to make informed financial decisions.

Secondly, Black Enterprise is a media and private equity firm focusing on entrepreneurship, investing, and personal finance. They offer financial education, advice columns, and practical advice for individuals interested in investing and entrepreneurship. They provide many resources, including webinars, magazines, and other digital content on Black wealth, business, and education.

Finally, the National Association of Black Accountants also provides resources to support and uplift Black individuals in financial education and planning. They offer mentorship, knowledge sharing, networking, and education and career development support. The organization is focused on empowering Black individuals with the resources they need to achieve financial stability and professional success.

These resources can provide valuable insights and education for Black individuals looking to improve their financial literacy and well-being. This knowledge can be invaluable in creating a more secure and prosperous future for themselves and their communities.

The root causes of economic inequality are complex and multifaceted, but they are woven into the fabric of U.S. history and society. Addressing this inequality requires a multidimensional approach that addresses systemic barriers (such as discriminatory lending practices and mass incarceration) and individual financial behavior (saving and investing). We can labor towards a more equitable and just economic future with coordinated efforts and a commitment to justice and equity.

CONTACT US

To Book John J as a Keynote Speaker

Visit Our Website:
www.adbmstateofmind.com

Write Us:
Address 272 Calhoun Station Pkwy
Suite C2244
Madison, MS 39110

24 Hours a Day, 7 Days a Week

Call Us:
Phone(844) 446-3623

Email john@adbmstateofmind.com

On Youtube @ ADBM State of Mind

Made in the USA
Columbia, SC
24 July 2023